# Adventures of Potato Head & Stick Girl

# Being Different

Amy Clapham

Illustrations by Haji Pajamas

One bright and early morning, Potato Head wanted to go for a walk on the beach.

Potato Head was a very curious dog and always loved to go to the beach because there were things to explore and see.

Stick Girl, Potato Head's
human, was still
sleeping, so it
took some really wet
kisses and snuggles in
her curly hair to get
her up!

At the beach there were lots of other dogs playing around.  One dog caught Potato Head's attention.

While Potato Head's fur was yellow and really fluffy, this dog's fur was as black as night, long and smooth. There was something else different about this dog, too.  She was missing a leg.

Potato Head walked
up to her and asked
her name.  Her name
was Lola.
Lola was able to
run and play in
the water, just like
the dogs with four legs.

Potato Head
wondered what
happened to
Lola, but was
afraid to ask.

Stick Girl saw that something was bothering Potato Head. After talking with him, Stick Girl learned that Potato Head was afraid. Stick Girl told him that he shouldn't be afraid, that if Lola didn't want to talk about her missing leg, she would say so.

Potato Head got up
the courage to ask
Lola and surprise - Lola
wasn't afraid to
talk about her
leg at all!

Potato Head found out that Lola had been very sick and because of her illness, lost a leg.  Lola was sad that she lost her leg, but very happy and thankful she could still come to the beach and play.

After a very long day
playing at the
beach, Potato Head
and Lola said
goodbye.  He told
her that she had
taught him a
very important lesson.

Just because someone
is different, doesn't
mean you should
be afraid of them.
You never know
what you may have
in common.

Potato Head and
Lola became
best friends.

Stick Girl was very
proud of Potato Head.
He put aside his fears
and because of that,
he made a friend
for life.

The End.

www.ingramcontent.com/pod-product-compliance
Lightning Source LLC
Chambersburg PA
CBHW041240040426
42445CB00004B/101

9780692630709